A Visit to BRAZIL

by Hermione Redshaw

Minneapolis, Minnesota

Credits

All images are courtesy of Shutterstock.com, unless otherwise specified. With thanks to Getty Images, Thinkstock Photo, and iStockphoto.

Cover – Maarten Zeehandelaar, marchello74. 2 – SJ Travel Photo and Video. 4–5 – Alexandre Rotenberg, Valik. 6–7 – VectorforPro, 061 Filmes. 8–9 – Edson J Ferreira, jocaphoto. 10–11 – Pavel Ilyukhin, DihandraPinheiro. 12–13 – Celso Pupo. 14–15 – Nelson Antoine, Marcos Amend. 16–17 – Iurii Dzivinskyi, slalomgigantei. 18–19 – MDI, lazyllamat. 20–21 – Curioso. Photography, Mark Green. 22–23 – Cacio Murilo, Paulo Vilela.

Library of Congress Cataloging-in-Publication Data is available at www.loc.gov or upon request from the publisher.

ISBN: 979-8-88509-369-9 (hardcover)
ISBN: 979-8-88509-491-7 (paperback)
ISBN: 979-8-88509-606-5 (ebook)

For more information, write to Bearport Publishing, 5357 Penn Avenue South, Minneapolis, MN 55419.

CONTENTS

COUNTRY TO COUNTRY

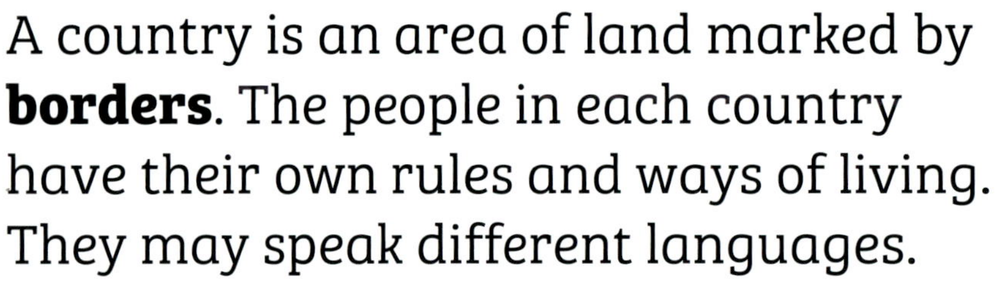

A country is an area of land marked by **borders**. The people in each country have their own rules and ways of living. They may speak different languages.

Which country do you live in?

Each country around the world has its own interesting things to see and do. Let's take a trip to visit a country and learn more!

TODAY'S TRIP IS TO
BRAZIL!

Brazil is a country in the **continent** of South America.

FACT FILE
Capital city: Brasília
Main language: Portuguese
Currency: Brazilian real
Flag:
ORDEM E PROGRESSO
Currency is the type of money that is used in a country.

BRASÍLIA

We'll start our trip in Brasília! This city was built in an empty **desert** in 1960. Today, Brasília is known for having many modern-style buildings.

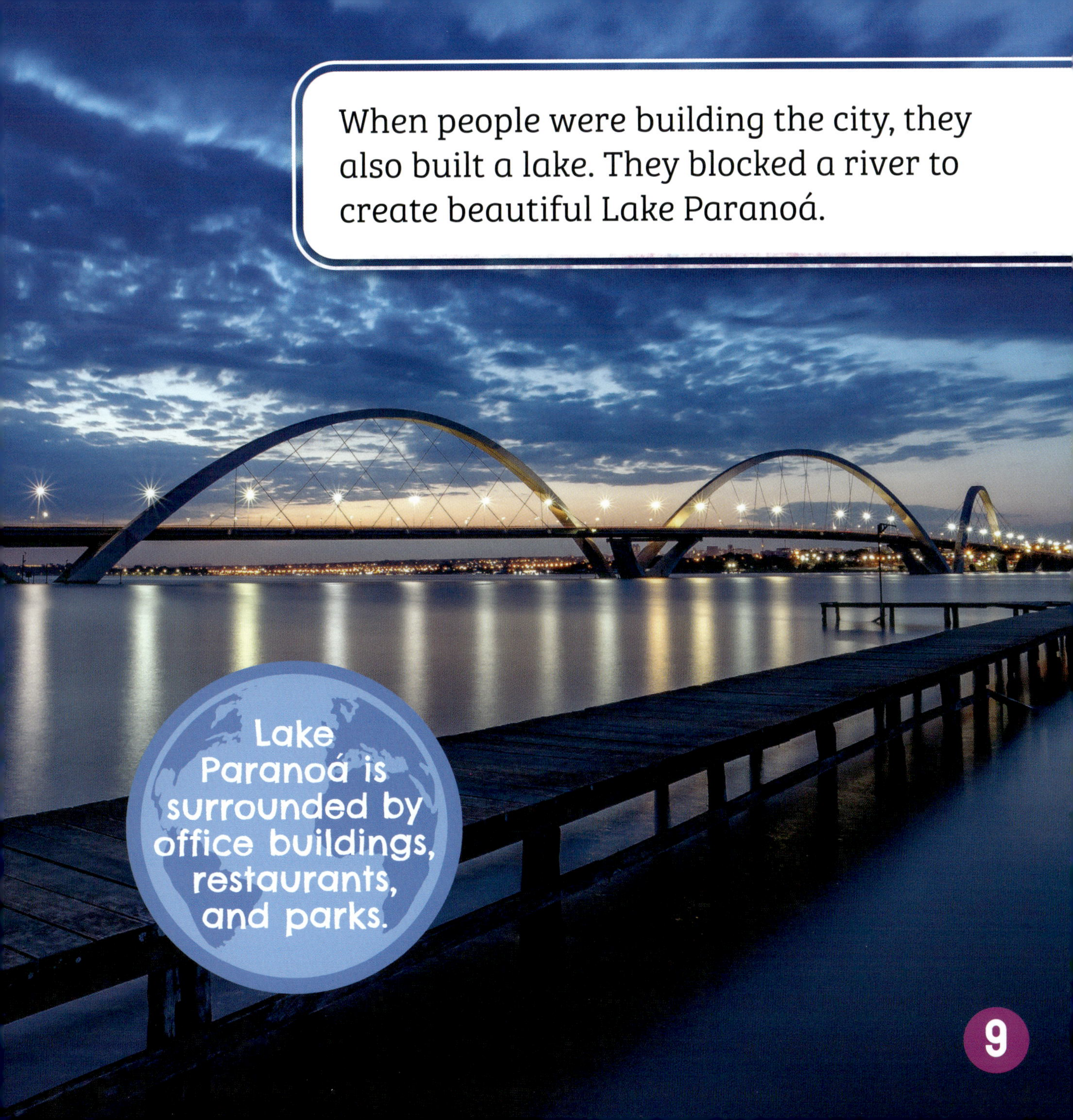

When people were building the city, they also built a lake. They blocked a river to create beautiful Lake Paranoá.

Lake Paranoá is surrounded by office buildings, restaurants, and parks.

SÃO PAULO

Brazil is home to people from all over the world. One place where we can see this is the country's biggest city, São Paulo.

In São Paulo, there is a **district** called Liberdade, which was started by people from Japan. The city also has Italian and German areas.

CARNIVAL

Let's celebrate! One of this country's biggest **festivals** is the Carnival of Brazil. It happens over six days in February.

Each part of the country celebrates Carnival a little differently. Many have dances and parades. People often wear colorful costumes.

MUSIC AND ART

Music is an important part of life in Brazil. Many types of music started in Brazil, including samba and bossa nova.

Brazil also has lots of art. Some of the country's most important art pieces are thousands of years old. They are cave paintings, pottery, and statues.

CHRIST THE REDEEMER STATUE

One of Brazil's famous statues is called Christ the Redeemer. It shows Jesus Christ, who is the central figure of Christianity, the main religion in Brazil.

This huge statue is about 100 feet (30 m) tall and is made of stone and concrete. It sits at the top of a mountain overlooking the city of Rio de Janeiro.

The statue was designed and built to be a **symbol** of peace.

SOCCER

Ready to play? The most popular sport in Brazil is soccer. But in Brazil, soccer is called football! The country's team has won five World Cups—the most of any country in the world.

Soccer came to Brazil in the 1800s. People who traveled from Scotland and England taught the sport to people in Brazil. Soon, soccer became a big part of Brazilian life.

AMAZON RAIN FOREST

This rain forest includes the Amazon River, which is the second-longest river in the world.

Next, let's leave the cities and head into nature. The Amazon is the world's largest tropical rain forest. Almost half of it is in Brazil.

The Amazon is home to thousands of animals, including jaguars, harpy eagles, and pink river dolphins. Some of these are not found anywhere else in the world.

BEFORE YOU GO

If you missed Carnival, there is another festival throughout June called Junina. During Junina, people dress in **traditional** clothing. They do a dance called the *quadrilha* and listen to music called *forró*.

And we can't forget to grab a bite to eat! Try some delicious *feijoada*. This black bean stew with beef and pork is the **national** dish of Brazil.

GLOSSARY

borders lines that show where one place ends and another begins

continent one of the world's seven large land masses

desert an area of very dry land that is usually hot and covered with sand or rocks

district a special area within a city

festivals events for lots of people to come together and celebrate

national something relating to an entire country

symbol something that stands for something else

traditional relating to something that a group of people has done for many years